MW01536129

Learning Tree
1 2 3

Whales

By Hannah E. Glease
Illustrated by George Thompson

CHERRYTREE BOOKS

Read this book and try to answer the questions. Ask an adult or an older friend to tell you if your answers are right or to help you if you find the questions difficult. Often there is more than one answer to a question.

A Cherrytree Book

Designed and produced by
A S Publishing

First published 1991
by Cherrytree Press Ltd
a subsidiary of
The Chivers Company Ltd
Windsor Bridge Road
Bath, Avon BA2 3AX

Copyright © Cherrytree Press Ltd 1991

British Library Cataloguing in Publication Data
Glease, Hannah E.
  Whales.
  1. Whales
  I. Title   II. Thompson, George   III. Series
  599.5

  ISBN 0-7451-5153-1

Printed and bound in Italy by L.E.G.O. s.p.a., Vicenza

This is a blue whale.
It lives in the sea.
It is the largest animal in the world.

minke whale

A blue whale is seven times the size of an
elephant.
Not all whales are so big.
A minke whale is smaller than a blue whale.

blue whale

pigmy sperm whale

A minke whale is the size of about two
elephants.
Other whales are even smaller.
Some are no bigger than a person.

tail – moved up and down
for swimming

blowhole – for
breathing

ears – hidden
beneath the
whale's skin

skin – smooth and
without hair

barnacles – small
animals that live
on the whale's skin

flippers – like
hands but
with no fingers

eyes – whales
have good
eyesight

mouth – whales
eat other animals

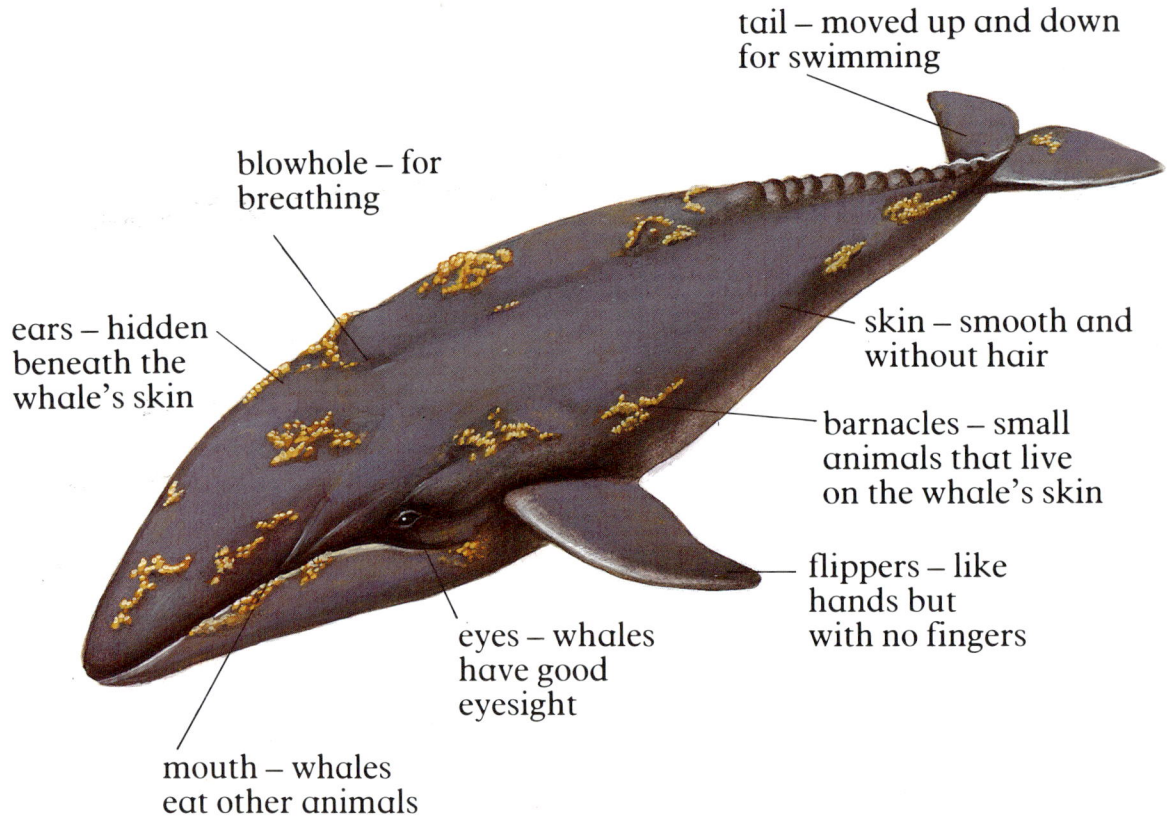

Whales look like big fish.
But they are not fish.
They are mammals like horses, cats and people.
This is a grey whale.

Fish have gills and can breathe underwater.
Whales have to breathe air at the surface.
They breathe through their blowholes.
When they breathe they make a spout of water.

Fish lay eggs. Whales have babies.
A baby whale is called a calf.
The mother whale gives birth underwater.
She pushes her calf to the surface so that it can
breathe.

The calf stays with its mother for some years.
At first it sucks milk from her body like a human baby.
When it is older, the calf eats the same food as its mother.

Some whales eat tiny shrimps called krill.
The shrimps float in the sea.

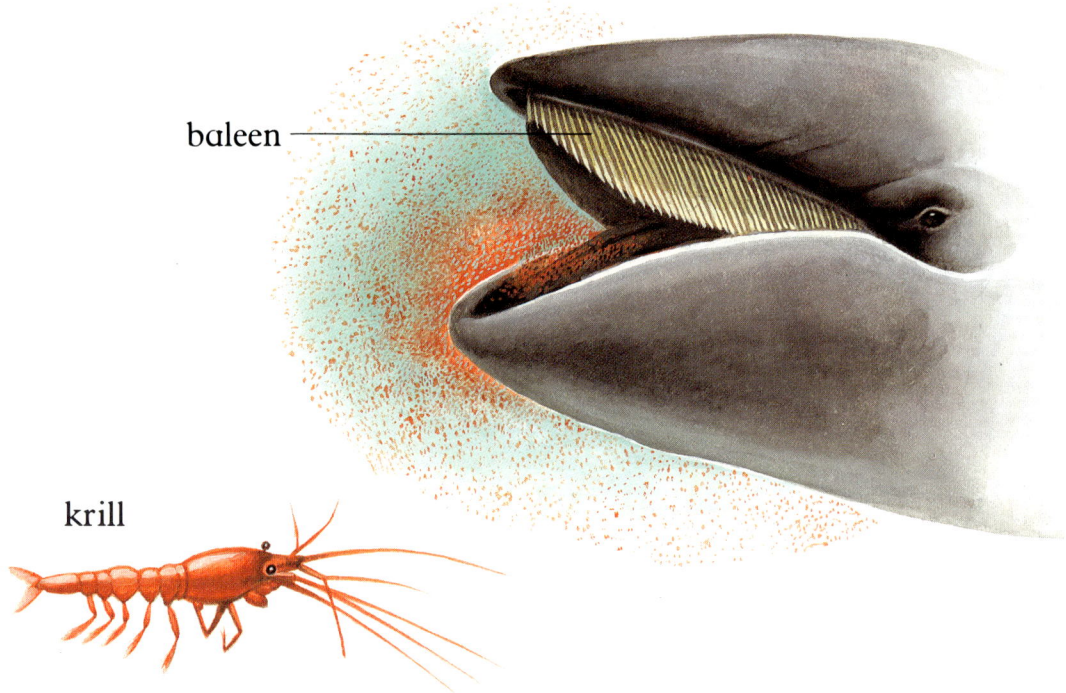

baleen

krill

The whale's mouth is like a strainer.
The whale takes a mouthful of water and krill.
Then it squeezes the water out of its mouth.
The strainer holds in the shrimps, but lets the
water through.
It is made of special bone called baleen.

Blue whales, grey whales and minke whales
all have baleen.
So do these whales.

Bryde's whale

humpback
whale

sei whale

bowhead whale

right
whale

11

Some whales have teeth.
They hunt for animals bigger than shrimps.

These whales like to eat fish and squid.
They cannot chew with their teeth.
They swallow their food whole.

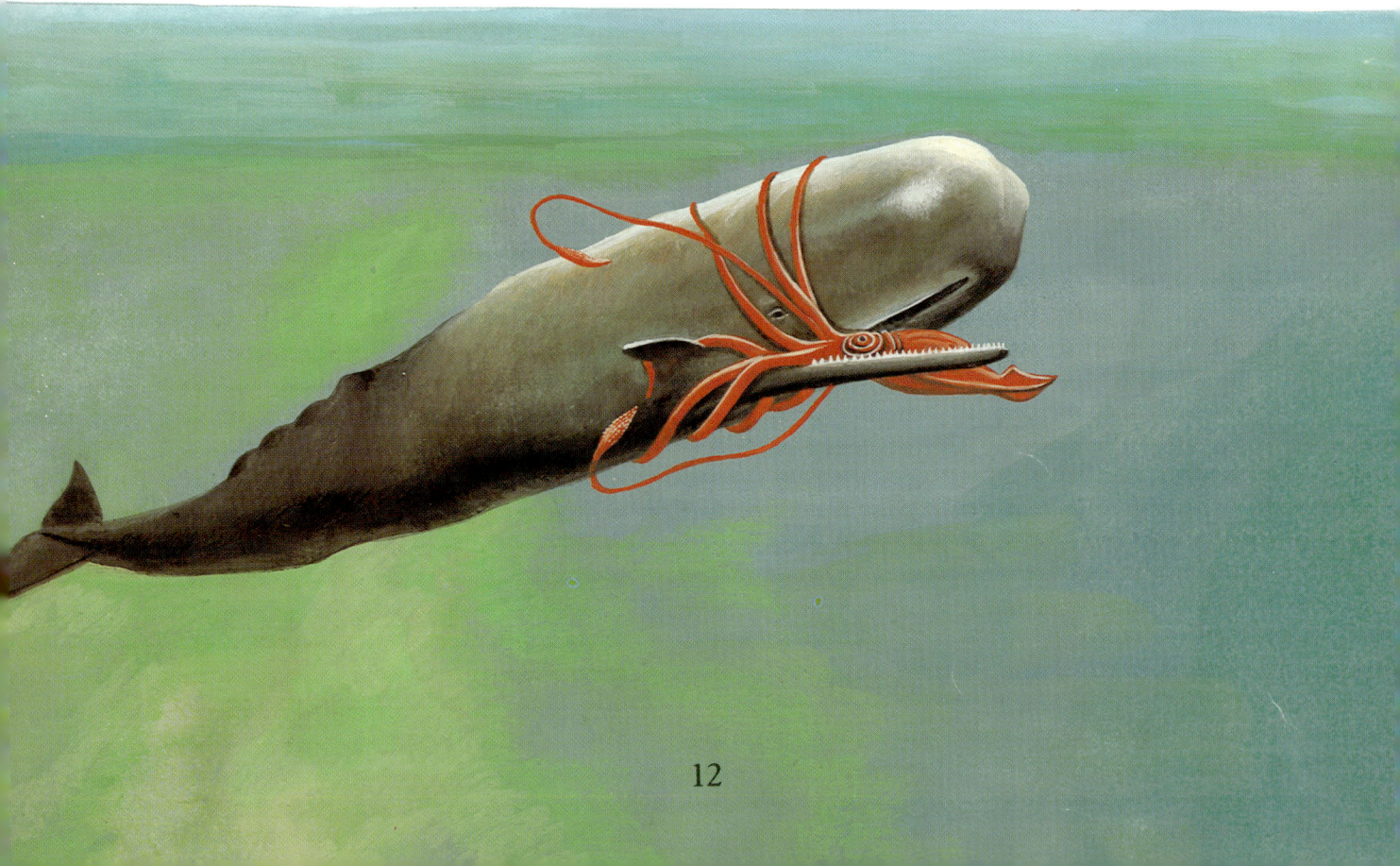

The sperm whale is the largest toothed whale.
It is the size of four elephants.
A sperm whale dives very deep when it is
hunting for squid.

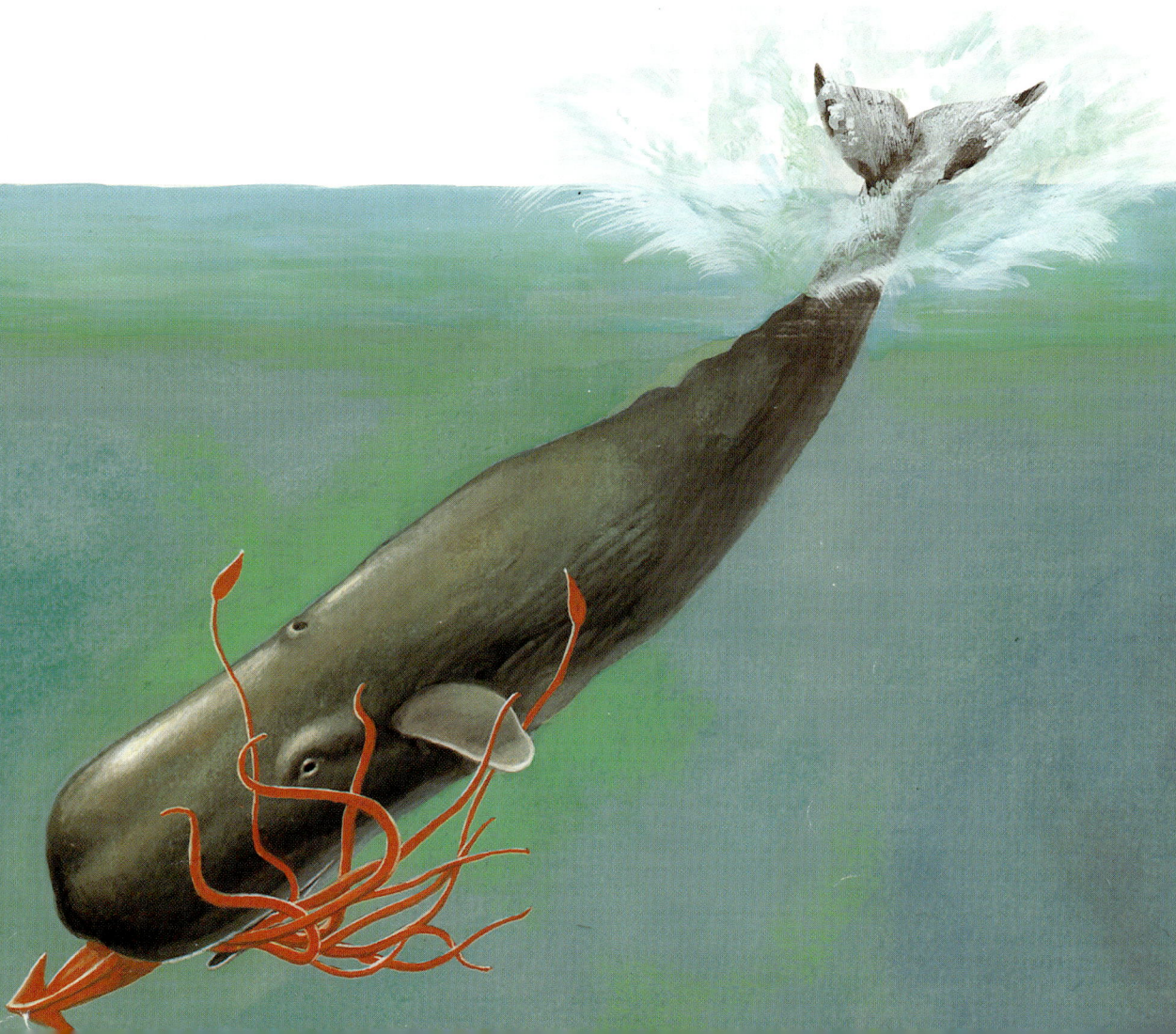

Killer whales are fierce hunters.
They like to eat salmon and other fish.
Sometimes they catch seals.

Killer whales live in family groups.
The groups are called pods.
All the whales in a pod hunt together.
Sometimes the pod divides into two groups.
One group drives fish towards the other group.

15

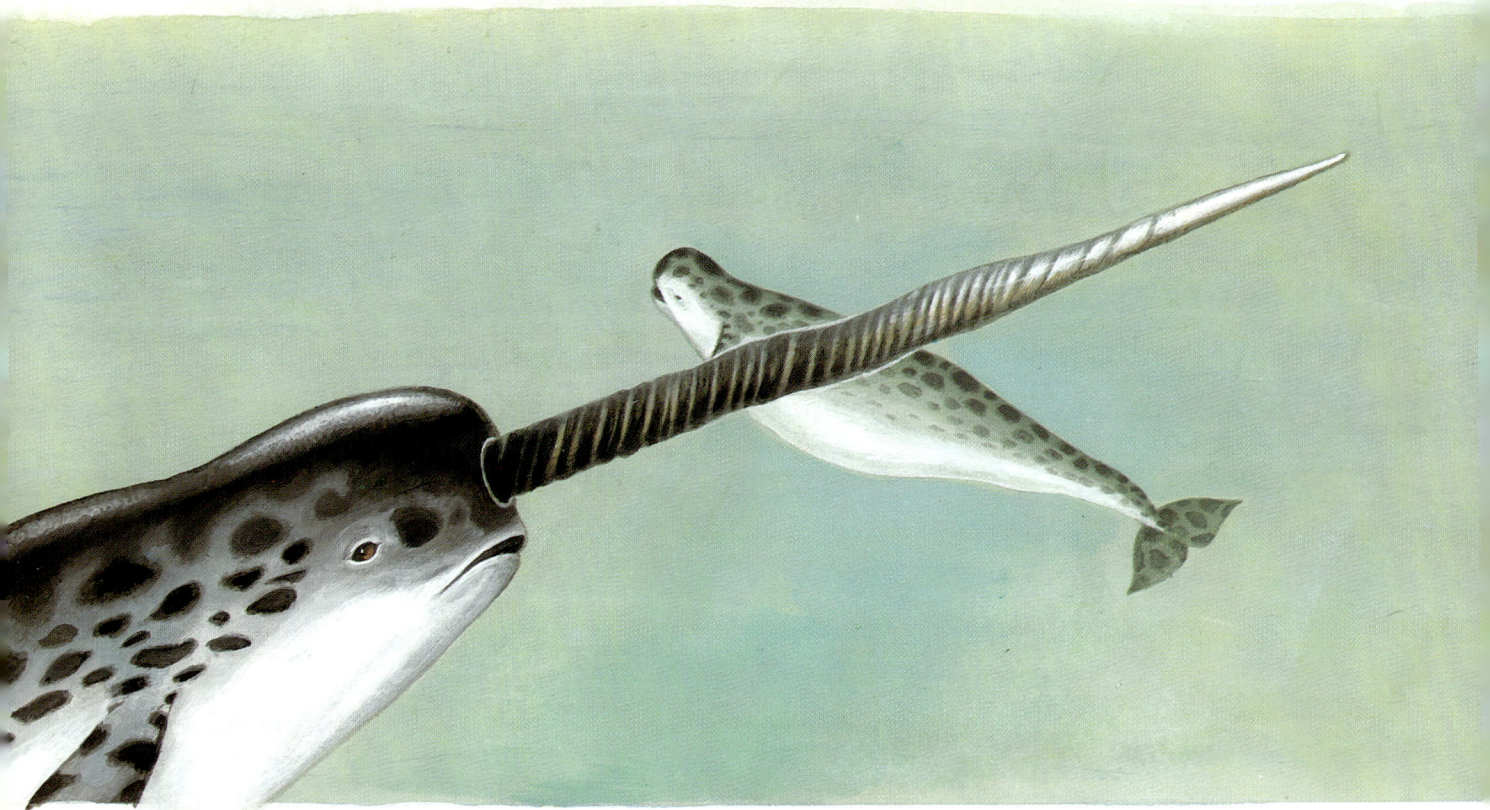

The narwhal has only two teeth.
One tooth is small and inside its mouth.
The other tooth sticks out like a horn.
The female narwhal has no teeth.

These little whales are dolphins.
They like to swim in front of ships and boats.
They leap in and out of the water.
These are bottle-nosed dolphins.

common porpoise

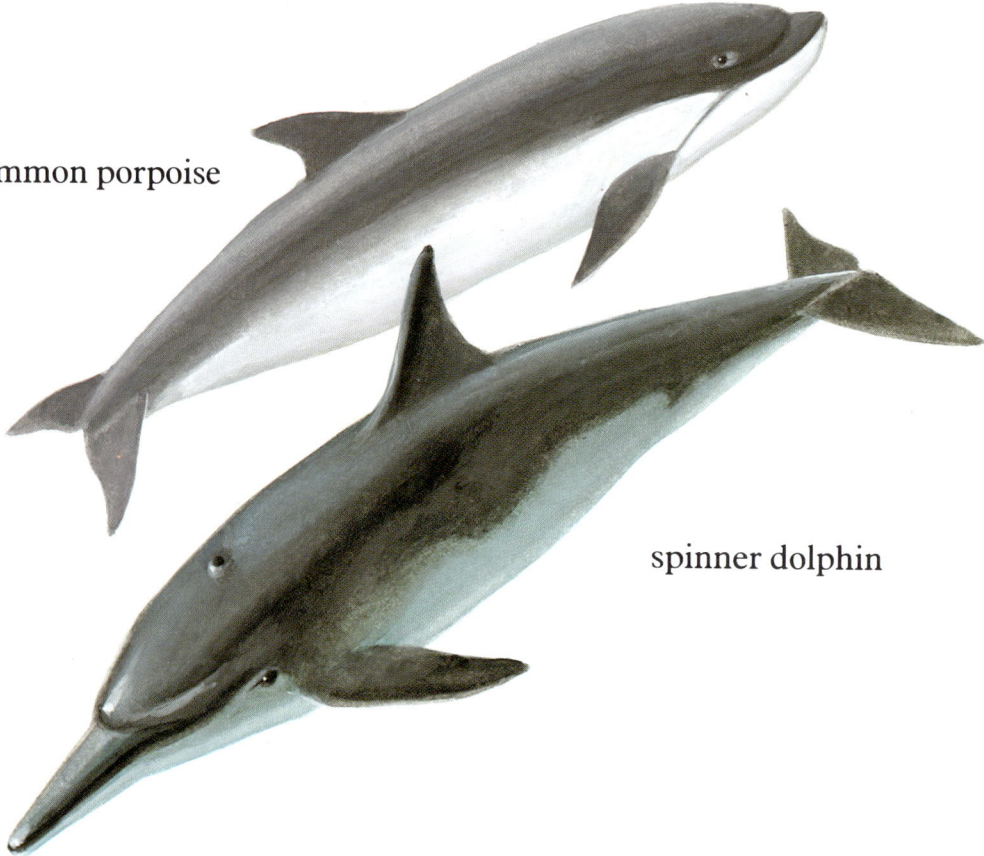

spinner dolphin

Dolphins and porpoises are small whales.
There are many different kinds.
Porpoises have rounded heads.
Dolphins have a pointed head with a beak.
They all have teeth.

Dolphins are clever and friendly animals.
They help each other if they are hurt.
Sometimes they help people as well.

Once people hunted whales for meat and oil.
Millions of whales were killed.
Some kinds of whale almost died out.
Now most whale hunting is banned but
whales are still in danger.

More about whales

Where whales live
Whales live in the sea in all parts of the world. Some whales live in the cold seas of the Arctic and around Antarctica. Other whales live in the warm seas near tropical countries. Altogether, there are more than 80 different kinds of whale, porpoise and dolphin.

Blubber
Whales have a thick layer of fat beneath their skin. This whale fat is called blubber. The layer of blubber keeps whales warm when they are swimming in cold water. Seals also have a layer of blubber.

Breathing
Whales swim underwater, but come to the surface to breathe. Most whales take a breath about every 10 or 15 minutes. The sperm whale, which dives very deep, can stay underwater for more than an hour.

Fish tails
Fish have an upright tail. They swim by moving their tail from side to side. Whales have a flat tail. They swim by moving their tail up and down.

Big baby
A blue whale calf is the biggest baby in the world. When it is born the calf weighs about seven tonnes. An adult blue whale weighs about 150 tonnes and lives for about 50 years.

Gentle giants
Most whales are very gentle and peaceful animals. They spend their whole lives far out at sea. Some whales even sing to each other underwater. The killer whale is a fierce hunter. But there are no records of a killer whale ever hurting a person.

Unicorn's horn
Once people believed that there was a magical beast called a unicorn. It was like a beautiful horse and it had a long horn on its head. People who saw a horn from a narwhal thought it must have come from a unicorn.

1

1 Where do whales live?

2 What is the biggest animal in the world?

3 Are whales fish?

4 Can whales breathe underwater?

5 Does a whale lay eggs?

6 What is a baby whale called?

7 What do baby whales feed on?

8 Can you draw a picture of a whale?

2

9 Can you write down the names of three different kinds of whale?

10 Why is a whale's blowhole on top of its head?

11 Why do mother whales push their calves to the surface?

12 Do whales have legs and arms?

13 How do whales catch the shrimps that they eat?

14 Name three whales that have baleen.

15 What do sperm whales eat?

16 What is different about the way in which whales and fish swim?

17 What kind of animals are whales? Are they insects, fish or mammals?

3

18 Make a whale notebook. Put your drawings and the answers to these questions in it. Think of other questions to ask about whales. Put these in your notebook.

19 What kind of whale lives in groups called pods?

20 What is the difference between a baleen whale and a toothed whale?

21 Can you name three kinds of toothed whale?

22 What kind of whale is bigger than a blue whale?

23 Why are a whale's ears hidden under its skin?

24 What kind of whale dives the deepest?

25 What is a narwhal's horn?

26 How much bigger is a blue whale than an elephant? How big is a minke whale?

27 Why do whales sing to each other? What do you think they sing about?

28 What sorts of sounds do you think whales make? Can you make whale sounds?

29 Do dolphins and porpoises have the same shape?

30 Why do dolphins help each other?

31 How could a dolphin help a person? What kinds of people could dolphins help?

32 Why did people kill whales?

33 Do you think people should kill whales and dolphins?

Index

Antarctica 21
Arctic 21
baleen 10, 11
barnacles 6
birth 8
blowhole 6, 7
blubber 21
blue whale 3, 4, 5, 11, 21
bowhead whale 11
breathing 6, 7, 8, 21
Bryde's whale 11
calf 8, 9, 21
cats 6
dolphins 17, 18, 19
ears 6
elephant 4, 5, 13
eyes 6
feeding 9, 10, 12

fish 6, 7, 8, 12, 14, 15, 21
flippers 6
gentleness 21
gills 7
grey whale 6-11
horses 6
humpback whale 11
hunting whales 20
killer whales 14, 15, 21
krill 10
mammals 6
milk 9
minke whale 4, 11
mouth 6, 10
narwhal 16, 21
people 6, 19
pigmy sperm whale 5

pod 15
porpoises 18
right whale 11
salmon 14
seals 14
sei whale 11
shrimps 10, 12
singing 21
size of whales 3, 4, 5, 13
skin 6
sperm whale 13
squid 12, 13
tail 6
teeth 12
toothed whales 12-19
unicorn's horn 21
where whales live 21